A Bit of a Shambles

CW01425948

Other Spirals Titles

Stories

Jim Alderson
Crash in the Jungle
The Witch Princess

Jan Carew
Death Comes to the Circus
Footprints in the Sand

Barbara Catchpole
Laura Called

Susan Duberley
The Ring

Keith Fletcher and Susan Duberley
Nightmare lake

John Goodwin
Dead-end Job
Ghost Train

Paul Groves
Not that I'm Work-shy
The Third Climber

Anita Jackson
The Actor
The Austin Seven
Bennet Manor
Dreams
The Ear
A Game of Life or Death
No Rent to Pay

Paul Jennings
Eye of Evil
Maggot

Margaret Loxton
The Dark Shadow

Patrick Nobes
Ghost Writer

David Orme
City of the Roborgs
The Haunted Asteroids

Kevin Philbin
Summer of the Werewolf

Julie Taylor
Spiders

John Townsend
Beware the Morris Minor
Fame and Fortune
Night Beast
SOS
A Minute to Kill

David Walke
Dollars in the Dust

Plays

Jan Carew
Computer Killer
No Entry
Time Loop

John Godfrey
When I Count to Three

Nigel Grey
An Earwig in the Ear

Paul Groves
Tell Me Where it Hurts

Barbara Mitchelhill
Punchlines
The Ramsbottoms at Home

Madeline Sotheby
Hard Time at Batwing Hall

John Townsend
Breaking the Ice
Cheer and Groan
Cowboys, Jelly and Custard
The End of the Line
Hanging by a Fred
The Lighthouse Keeper's Secret
Making a Splash
Murder at Muckleby Manor
Over and Out
Taking the Plunge

David Walke
The Bungle Gang Strike Again
The Good, the Bad and the Bungle
Package Holiday

A Bit of a Shambles

John Townsend

Stanley Thornes (Publishers) Ltd

First published in 1997 by:
Stanley Thornes (Publishers) Ltd
Ellenborough House
Wellington Street
CHELTENHAM GL50 1YW
England

97 98 99 00 01 / 10 9 8 7 6 5 4 3 2 1

A catalogue record for this book is available from the British Library.

ISBN 0–7487–3085–0

Cover artwork by Jacqueline East
Typeset by Tech-Set, Gateshead
Printed and bound in Great Britain at Martin's The Printers, Berwick

Contents

Five short plays for two parts about Mix-ups, Mess-ups and Muddles!

A Leap in the Dark

2 parts:
In – Someone on the inside of the window
Out – Someone on the outside, on the window ledge

In	*[Jumping up from the armchair]* Excuse me! Hey, you! Oi, you out there . . . *[Opens window]* What do you think you're doing out there on my window ledge?
Out	Nothing. Nothing at all. Yet.
In	Do you live in these flats? Have you lost your key or something?
Out	No. Not at all.
In	Are you lost?
Out	No. Oh no. I'm not lost. I know where I'm going.
In	Then I hope you don't mind me asking . . . but what are you doing out there on my window ledge on a foggy night like this?
Out	Yes, it's very foggy, isn't it?
In	You gave me the shock of my life.

Out	Sorry.
In	I pulled back the curtains to see if the fog had gone. I sat down for a cup of tea and what did I see? A pair of legs at my window!
Out	I climbed out of the skylight by the lift in the hall.
In	Well, you'd better come in.
Out	No thanks.
In	You're not a burglar, I hope.
Out	No. Leave me alone.
In	Or the window cleaner? The window cleaner doesn't usually come at night. Mind you, it could take all night to clean the windows in this block. Over twenty floors in these flats, you know.
Out	That's why I came. Where it's very high. Now leave me alone.
In	Leave you alone? You could hurt yourself out there.
Out	That's right.
In	Just think if you fell off. In this fog we'd never find you.
Out	That's why I'm here.
In	You what?

Out	I don't want to be found. I'm going to kill myself. I hate life. I can't go on.
In	Oh dear. I hope it's nothing I've said. Did I upset you?
Out	I've had enough.
In	Well, try to look on the bright side. Let me cheer you up a bit. Er . . . let me tell you a joke or something. Let me think . . .
Out	Please don't bother. I hate jokes.
In	Isn't it funny how you can never think of a good joke when you need it?
Out	I just want to be alone.
In	Now, there was this vicar at a funeral . . . oh dear, maybe not!
Out	I was just about to jump when you opened the window.
In	No, no, not yet. Another joke. Let me make you laugh.
Out	No . . . please . . . aaaaah!
In	Oh dear, what's the matter?
Out	I slipped. For an awful moment I thought I was going.

8

In	How about a good riddle to take your mind off things? Now then, what do you get if you cross an elephant with a peanut butter sandwich?
Out	I don't know and I don't care.
In	You are down in the dumps, aren't you? Well how about this one . . . you'll kill yourself laughing with this . . . Oh, sorry.
Out	You're not doing me any good.
In	Can I fetch you a mug of soup? It's a terrible night out there. A torch might be a help so you can see where you're going. So you can have a little peep before you hit the ground.
Out	Please leave me. I don't want to see. That's the whole point.
In	Are you sure you don't want a nice little chat about things?
Out	There's nothing to say. It's been the worst day of my life. My job is getting me down. Spurs have lost at home again. Everyone hates me. My spots are getting worse and I'm ugly. Even the cat has run off with the ginger tom from next door. I sent my photo to *The Lonely Hearts Club* but they sent it back and said they weren't that lonely. Life just isn't worth living. So it's goodbye world . . . and don't think you can stop me.

9

In	I wouldn't dream of it. I'll give you a hand if you like.
Out	Tell me. Be honest. Do you think I'm fat and ugly?
In	Of course not. You're not fat at all.
Out	But I'm ugly, aren't I?
In	Not really. Only in places. Anyway, it's too dark to tell. Listen, could you do something for me?
Out	Don't think you can talk me out of this.
In	I wouldn't dream of it. You stay where you are. I just want to give you something?
Out	I don't think a prayer book will be any help to me now.
In	I was thinking of a rag and bucket of water.
Out	Why? How will that help me in my hour of need?
In	It won't, but I've been trying to clean those windows for ages and I just can't reach from here.
Out	You want me to stand on this narrow ledge and wipe your windows?
In	Yes please. That would be very good of you.
Out	You must be mad. I could fall and break my neck.

In	I thought that's what you wanted. Look, if you do feel yourself slipping, could you please try to fall in a straight line and don't smear the glass.
Out	I've got enough on my mind without worrying about your windows.
In	And I've got enough on my windows without worrying about your mind. Don't jump about on that bit of ledge. It's rotting. If you break it, it will cost a fortune to mend.
Out	What about me? You don't care about me at all, do you?
In	Of course. I worry about the mess you'll make when you jump.
Out	Don't. Stop it. Don't talk about it. I can't stand heights.
In	Then why are you out there on my window ledge?
Out	The only reason I'm out here tonight is because of the fog. Then I can't see the ground. It's better that way.
In	You mean you'll just leap out in the dark and wait for the splat?
Out	Don't say that.
In	As you fly through the air will you close your eyes and wait to be smashed to bits on the path below?

Out	Stop it. Stop it. Think about my feelings.
In	Think about us who have to pick you up – all the bits. Would you like a cup of tea? The kettle is boiling.
Out	No. Now please leave me alone.
In	Aren't you going to leave a message for the world? What shall I tell the papers?
Out	There is one thing you can do for me before I go.
In	Yes? What is it? How can I help?
Out	Put me out of my misery.
In	How? What do you want me to do? Shall I give you a little push? Yes, I can just about reach.
Out	No! No, please. Help, you'll kill me. Help, police!
In	Well, what's all the fuss about, then?
Out	You just don't understand, do you? You lot are all the same. Suicide isn't easy, you know. You only die once and I want to make a good job of it. Now, please – tell me the one thing I'm dying to know.
In	Yes, what is it?
Out	What is the answer?
In	To life?

Out	No – your riddle. What do you get if you cross an elephant with a peanut butter sandwich?
In	Oh, that's simple. You get a sandwich that never forgets or you get an elephant that sticks to the roof of your mouth!
Out	That's terrible. Now you've made up my mind for me. I can't live with that sort of rubbish . . . Here goes . . .
In	Was it something I said?
Out	AAAAAAAH! *[Jumps]*
In	*[Calling down out of the window]* I'll just go and get you that cup of tea. I can pop out and tell you a few more jokes as well. Listen, here's a good one . . . and it's true . . . we're only on the ground floor!

Just a Trim

2 parts:
Hairdresser, Customer

Scene: *In a hairdressing salon*

Hairdresser	Next please.
Customer	Good. I'm in a bit of a hurry.
Hairdresser	Hello. And what can I do for you?
Customer	Just a check-up, really.
Hairdresser	I beg your pardon?
Customer	Just a quick look and a bit of a poke about. Make sure no fillings have fallen out. Maybe a bit of a polish.
Hairdresser	Fillings?
Customer	I had a bit of a twinge in one tooth last week . . .
Hairdresser	Er – I think you must have made a mistake.
Customer	Oh no, I'm quite sure it was last week. Yes, it was Monday . . .
Hairdresser	I'm not a dentist.
Customer	It was the day I got these glasses fixed. No, I tell a lie, it was the Tuesday, the day the bin men call. I remember now because I hopped

in the back of the dust cart. I thought it was the bus.

Hairdresser	I am a hairdresser.
Customer	Between you and me, I think they gave me the wrong glasses. I haven't been able to see much since then.
Hairdresser	This is a hair salon.
Customer	I went back to complain. Oh yes, I made a great fuss I can tell you. I stormed in and gave them a piece of my mind.
Hairdresser	Well, didn't they change them for you?
Customer	No. They didn't seem to understand.
Hairdresser	Why was that?
Customer	I was in the fish shop. To be honest, I can see better without them. Now then, shall I open wide? [*Opens mouth*] How's that. Pass the mouth wash will you?
Hairdresser	I could give you a cup of coffee.
Customer	What a good idea. Much better than that horrid pink stuff. I must say, the dentist has never put a sheet round me before. Is this a new idea?
Hairdresser	It's for your haircut.

Customer	A what?
Hairdresser	A haircut. This is a salon.
Customer	Well fancy that! A dentist who gives a haircut at the same time. What a good idea to get it all over in one go! Do you cut toe nails as well?
Hairdresser	I'm afraid not. I don't think you've got the right idea.
Customer	Then just give me a bit of a trim-up, will you?
Hairdresser	There is one little problem.
Customer	Not too much off the top.
Hairdresser	This won't be easy.
Customer	Just a snip here and a brush there.
Hairdresser	There is a bit of a snag.
Customer	It could do with a wash as well while you're at it.
Hairdresser	A bit of a hiccup.
Customer	And a blow dry. I wouldn't mind a few highlights.
Hairdresser	Highlights?
Customer	Or tram lines. Maybe a few blond tints. What do you think?

Hairdresser	I don't really think so.
Customer	Or what about lots of curls? Maybe a few waves.
Hairdresser	That wouldn't be too wise.
Customer	What about gel? Get it to stand up a bit.
Hairdresser	I don't think so, somehow.
Customer	Why not? You must be able to spice it up a bit.
Hairdresser	Not really. It won't be that easy.
Customer	Just give it a bit of bounce.
Hairdresser	That's out of the question, I'm afraid.
Customer	Make me look years younger.
Hairdresser	I don't think I can do that.
Customer	Why ever not? What is the world coming to? What is stopping you?
Hairdresser	Just a slight problem. A minor hitch.
Customer	Well, whatever is it?
Hairdresser	You.
Customer	Me?
Hairdresser	Yes. You're bald.
Customer	What?

Hairdresser	You're . . . without. You're hairless. You're a . . . non-haired person. To be honest, you're as bald as an egg!
Customer	Bald?
Hairdresser	Like a snooker ball. I think you were right earlier when you asked for a polish. I could shine things up for you if you like!
Customer	But what about curls and lovely waves?
Hairdresser	No waves, I'm afraid – the whole tide's gone out! All you can do now is wave goodbye!
Customer	Rubbish. There used to be three fine healthy hairs on my head. You take a closer look. Can you see them?
Hairdresser	Er . . . oh yes. I see what you mean. Three hairs. Three little shoots.
Customer	Right then, I'd like them tidied up a bit. Give them style.
Hairdresser	I see. Very well. Would you like a side parting?
Customer	Yes. On the left. Careful not to split the ends.
Hairdresser	I'll comb this one on this side and the other two over this side. There – how's that?
Customer	Yes, that feels a lot smarter. By the way, don't look now but have you noticed that odd person staring at us?

Hairdresser	No – where?
Customer	Just there in front of us. I don't like the look of that face. Rather ugly if you ask me.
Hairdresser	That's the mirror.
Customer	I really must get these glasses changed!
Hairdresser	Oh dear – I'm very sorry . . . it's your hair!
Customer	What about it? Has it grown?
Hairdresser	One of them just fell out. It just came away on the comb. I've got some glue somewhere . . .
Customer	Darn it. You'll just have to give me a centre parting now.
Hairdresser	Would you like some hair spray to keep them in place?
Customer	Yes, but first of all you could dry them. I've been out in the rain so they could do with a quick blow under the dryer.
Hairdresser	Certainly – or I could just breathe on them for you if you like!
Customer	No – I'll just stick my head up under this dryer and it won't take long. Just switch it on, will you?
Hairdresser	I'd rather not. That's the lamp shade you've put your head under.

Customer	I must change these glasses.
Hairdreser	Oh dear. Oh deary dear!
Customer	What's the matter?
Hairdresser	You won't believe this.
Customer	What?
Hairdresser	I'm afraid another hair has just dropped out. I'm very sorry. At least it will solve the dandruff problem!
Customer	Darn it! In that case I will go and take my custom elsewhere. I don't want any more harm done and I'm certainly not letting you get your hands on my teeth.
Hairdresser	I could put a spot of gel on the hair that's left if you like.
Customer	Don't be daft. I will look like a walking candle with a wick sticking up in the air. I've had enough. I will have to leave it looking untidy. I shall leave here looking a right scruff!
Hairdresser	Sorry about that. I won't charge for your haircut!
Customer	I should jolly well think not. And I'm not letting you look in my mouth. My teeth will be out on the floor before I know it! No, I'm not coming in here ever again. [Opens door] Goodbye.

Hairdresser	Goodbye! Oh dear. But I know you'll come back one day. I'm sure it won't be long before you come back here.
Customer	Well, that's just where you're wrong. I could safely bet you a hundred pounds I will never set foot in this room again.
Hairdresser	Done! Goodbye.
Customer	Goodbye! [*Slams door behind*]
Hairdresser	I'll take cash or a cheque.
Customer	[*Opens door and enters*] Have you got something to say?
Hairdresser	Yes – that's the cupboard you're in. A hundred pounds, please!
Customer	Certainly not! I really must get these glasses seen to. But now I'm off and don't you worry – I might be here today, but I certainly won't be here tomorrow.
Hairdresser	Not quite.
Customer	What do you mean – NOT QUITE?
Hairdresser	Well after all, in your case I think it's a matter of HAIR TODAY, GONE TOMORROW. Good afternoon!

Just Relax

Try recording these sound effects onto a cassette to play at the correct moment in the following play:

1 Car doors slamming

2 Car engine starting

3 Engine revving

4 Louder engine noises

5 CRASH! (e.g. dropping an empty biscuit tin)

6 Running water/splashing

7 Another CRASH – as before

8 Hissing (e.g. air being released from a balloon)

9 POP! (e.g. a balloon bursting)

10 A referee's whistle

11 A car horn

12 BANG and CRUNCH! (e.g. stamping on a cardboard box with plastic cups/spoons inside)

2 parts:

Adams (driving examiner), Bob (driver)

Scene: Outside in the street

Adams	Mr. Clarke?
Bob	Oh. Sorry? What? You made me jump.
Adams	Are you ready?
Bob	Ready? I was just looking. Smart car. Very nice.
Adams	You'd better get in.
Bob	In?
Adams	Of course. In you get.
Bob	Me? In here?
Adams	Well, it is time, Mr. Clarke. On the dot.
Bob	Time?
Adams	For your test. Time for your driving test.
Bob	Oh dear.
Adams	Don't be nervous. Relax. Just get in.
Bob	I don't want to. I don't think I should.
Adams	Just relax. Just pop in and sit in the driver's seat.
Bob	Oh no. I can't. I'm coming over all funny.

Adams	Don't worry about a thing. Relax. Now, in you get.

[*Sound effect 1: Doors slam*]

Bob	It's very posh in here.
Adams	I take it you haven't driven this car before. Just relax.
Bob	Will it take long?
Adams	No. Not long. Unless we go in the river . . . my little joke.
Bob	But I've got to be back at work in an hour. I can't be late.
Adams	Fine. Relax. I've got to be off by then as well. I'm off on holiday.
Bob	Where to?
Adams	Spain.
Bob	Is that right or left at the traffic lights?
Adams	No – that's where I'm going for my holiday. Just relax.
Bob	Oh, I see. What a relief. I thought that's where I had to drive to.
Adams	We go every year. Very nice beach.
Bob	I've got to catch a bus in half an hour.

Adams	And the hotel is very nice.
Bob	So I haven't got much time. I need to be quick.
Adams	Lovely swimming pool. Ever so warm.
Bob	But the thing is, I don't feel well. My head is all fizzy.
Adams	Hot sun each day.
Bob	I think it could be the bottle of sherry I had for breakfast.
Adams	Nice food.
Bob	I didn't mean to pour all of it on my cornflakes.
Adams	I can't wait to get on that plane. So you're lucky, I'm in a good mood!
Bob	Not after the gin on my Sugar Puffs.
Adams	I've got my passport and tickets with me. All safe.
Bob	And rum on my Coco-Pops.
Adams	So shall we start? Ready?
Bob	Start?
Adams	Yes. Start the car.
Bob	Do you think I should?
Adams	I can't test you if you don't! Just relax. Now, off we go.

Bob	Fine. If you say so. If that's what you want . . . er . . .
Adams	Relax. What's the matter?
Bob	I forget. How do you make it start?
Adams	Keys.
Bob	Oh, of course. How silly of me. Yes. Yes . . . er, where are they?
Adams	In the dashboard.
Bob	Oh, of course. How silly of me. Yes. Yes . . . er, where is it?
Adams	In front of you. Now just relax and start the engine.

[*Sound effect 2: Engine starts*]

Bob	Ooh, it's noisy, isn't it? It does my head in!
Adams	Just drive out onto the road and turn left.
Bob	Left?
Adams	Left.
Bob	Are you sure?
Adams	Of course I'm sure. Just relax.
Bob	Good. Fine. I just want to make sure. Only the thing is . . .
Adams	Just relax. What is it?

26

Bob	Just remind me.
Adams	Remind you what?
Bob	Left. Where is it? Which side? I forget.
Adams	You don't know? It's that side. Now – do relax.
Bob	Oh yes, I thought so. I just wanted to make sure.
Adams	Do you plan to change gear?
Bob	What?

[*Sound effect 3: Engine revving*]

Adams	To change gear. You need to change.
Bob	Don't you like this shirt, then?
Adams	GEAR! Change up!
Bob	Oh, I see. Sorry. I just wanted to make sure. Here goes . . .
Adams	Just relax.
Bob	What a bumpy road. We're jumping about like a kangaroo.
Adams	The clutch. Use the clutch!
Bob	Will that help?
Adams	You really must relax, Mr. Clarke.
Bob	Do you mind if I ask you something?

Adams	Just get on with it.
Bob	I forget . . . Which one of those things on the floor is the clutch?
Adams	WHAT? Don't you know it's the one on the left?
Bob	Oh, thanks. That's a great help.
Adams	This isn't going very well, is it? You must relax. You're all tight.
Bob	I feel very tight! Er . . . I hope you don't mind me asking this . . .
Adams	Now what?
Bob	I forget.
Adams	Relax. You forget what?
Bob	Which side is the right?
Adams	That's it! I've had enough.
Bob	I only wanted to make sure.
Adams	Stop the car.
Bob	Er . . . just remind me . . .
Adams	Over to the kerb . . .
Bob	Left or right?
Adams	Quick – pull over.
Bob	How do you mean?

Adams	Pull over. Do you hear? Pull over.
Bob	Oh, so it is.
Adams	What are you staring at?
Bob	Your pullover. It's very nice. Is it from Marks and Spencers?
Adams	Stop this car. Now. Stop! You're going faster.
Bob	Just remind me . . . which one of those things is the brake?
Adams	The middle one!
Bob	I just wanted to make sure.
Adams	Go on . . . stop it!
Bob	I hope you don't mind me asking but . . . which one is the middle?
Adams	What? Can't you tell the middle one out of three pedals?
Bob	Three? There are six down there.
Adams	Six?
Bob	Oh dear . . . and I've got four feet!
Adams	Four feet? I don't believe this. Now, stop this car.
Bob	I must be seeing double.
Adams	Double?

Bob	Double.
Adams	DOUBLE?
Bob	And I'm hearing an echo. It's that sherry. I'm in a bad way, aren't I?
Adams	Yes you are. Now stop this car and let me get out. Help!
Bob	Unless it's the gin. Might be the rum. Or the Coco-Pops.
Adams	Give me that steering wheel . . .

[*Sound effect 4: Louder engine noises – roaring!*]

Bob	Please don't do that, you made me panic.
Adams	What about me? Please, I beg you. Let me out.
Bob	Just relax. I'm getting the hang of this now.
Adams	I want to get out. I want to go on holiday. Please.
Bob	I can't see much through this windscreen.
Adams	It's rain. Turn on the wipers.
Bob	Is it this lever?
Adams	Aaaah! No, that tips my seat back. Look, here's a car park.
Bob	Really? How nice.
Adams	Please pull in. I want to go and catch my plane.

Bob	Here's the way in. Just relax. I'll drive straight in . . .
Adams	No – look out . . . it's coming down . . .
Bob	Yes, it's been raining all day.
Adams	Stop! That big metal bar is coming down. Look out!

[*Sound effect 5: Crash!*]

Bob	Oops.
Adams	Now look what you've done! Let me out of here!
Bob	I didn't know this was one of those cars where the roof goes back.
Adams	It wasn't. We've lost the whole roof. No . . . no . . . not in here. Stop!
Bob	Just relax. Gosh, it's really blowing up a storm now. Terrible weather.
Adams	We'll get soaked!
Bob	Have you ever seen rain like this?
Adams	Never. This is the car wash. Oh no, here it comes . . . AAAAH!

[*Sound effect 6: Water – slurping, sploshing and swishing!*]

Bob	Phew! Did that fluffy roller just do to you what it did to me?

Adams	I don't know but it will save me using dental floss for a while!
Bob	My teeth and gums are spotless.
Adams	Same here. So spotless, they've gone. So has my vest.
Bob	And my glasses . . . I can't see a thing now.
Adams	Then stop. Let me out. Let me live my life. Where are we going?
Bob	Down by Tescos. There's a short cut back to where we started. Relax.
Adams	I can't relax.
Bob	Why?
Adams	Because we're going IN Tescos. Mind that trolley!
Bob	We'll never get through the check-out.
Adams	Then use the fruit and veg stand as a roundabout, then exit. Oh no!

[*Sound effect 7: Crash and clatter*]

Bob	Just relax. Only tins of cat food. There you are, we're outside now.
Adams	I just want to get to the airport.
Bob	Terrible weather. Hail stones all over the place.

Adams	It's glass – from the window we've just gone through.
Bob	I can't think why we're bumping and jumping like this.
Adams	We're going down the steps into the subway. If you stop the car, I'll pay you £100.
Bob	Just relax. Nearly home. Just up the other side and through the park.
Adams	I need my holiday. All this stress. Please – take ALL my money. STOP!
Bob	How? How do you stop? This wall should help.
Adams	No . . . no . . . NO!

[*Sound effect 8: Crash and hiss*]

Bob	Hey, that's clever.
Adams	Mmmph . . . blbbbb . . . brrrfffff
Bob	I wish I could do that. You're very good with bubble gum.
Adams	Umph . . . glumph . . . brrrfffff
Bob	I've always wanted to blow a bubble like that.
Adams	Help . . . the air bag has gone off in my face!
Bob	Not to worry.
Adams	I can't see a thing.

Bob	Nor can I. Never mind. Just relax.
Adams	I'm choking on it. Help!
Bob	Don't worry. I've got a pin. Here we are.

[Sound effect 9: Pop!]

Adams	Aaah! I can't stand any more of this. Oh no – now I CAN see where we're going!
Bob	Kids today! Just look at them. They ought to know it's not safe here.
Adams	You can say that again!
Bob	Fancy playing with a ball in the middle of the street. Stupid kids!
Adams	Not really – it's the football field. And we're just going through the goal at 50 miles per hour with the referee upside down on the back seat. His shorts are stuck on the mirror and his underpants are on the gear stick.

[Sound effect 10: Whistle blows]

Bob	I think we lost him in the rose bed. We're nearly back now.
Adams	Can I open my eyes yet?
Bob	Here we are. Back to where we started. Just across this main road . . .
Adams	There's a bus. Look out!

[*Sound effect 11: Loud horn*]

Bob	That bus shouldn't be allowed out on the road.
Adams	It's not. It's parked at the bus station and now we're on the path.
Bob	Just relax. Where do you think I should park?
Adams	Over there next to my car . . . oh no, what have I said?

[*Sound effect 12: Crunch!*]

Bob	Was that car yours? It just came out at me.
Adams	What about the others? You've hit them all. But we're back! I'm safe!
Bob	Just relax. Why are you biting the steering wheel and hugging me?
Adams	Mr. Clarke, I'm afraid I have to tell you . . . YOU FAILED YOUR TEST!
Bob	Never mind. Not to worry. Nice ride. It was fun.
Adams	FUN? We nearly got killed. The town is in bits. Look at the mess!
Bob	There's just one question before I go off to work.
Adams	What is it, Mr. Clarke?
Bob	Why do you keep calling me Mr. Clarke?
Adams	You mean . . . you're NOT Mr. Clarke?

Bob	No – but he might be. The chap over there sobbing on the floor.
Adams	You mean the one eating his 'L' plates and ripping out his hair?
Bob	Could be. He keeps shouting about his car. This car!
Adams	But . . . I thought YOU were Mr. Clarke. You were just standing here . . .
Bob	I was looking at the car.
Adams	And I said to you, 'Hello, Mr. Clarke . . .'
Bob	I thought you were telling me YOUR name and asking me to go for a little spin in your car. I was only being friendly.
Adams	So you'd never driven before?
Bob	Never. Nothing like this.
Adams	Oh. Ah. Um.
Bob	We could keep it a secret.
Adams	The whole town has seen us! We've been through Tescos, the subway, across the football pitch, over the golf course and three times round the bus station. You've been drinking, you're seeing double and you're unfit to sit behind the wheel.

Bob	Does that matter?
Adams	And I let you drive someone else's car! It could mean prison . . .
Bob	For both of us?
Adams	Of course.
Bob	Oh. It's just that this car is nothing like the machine I use at work.
Adams	I think I might fly to Spain and stay there!
Bob	And me!
Adams	Not with me you're not! I never want to see you again. Never.
Bob	Well, that's where you're wrong.
Adams	I'm going now. My flight is due soon.
Bob	Just relax. Is it the 5.38 flight to Madrid you are going on?
Adams	Yes, but I'm not letting you on it. I'll buy up all the spare seats!
Bob	Not mine, you won't. They'll save me my seat. It's where I work.
Adams	Work? You? No, please . . . aaah!
Bob	That's right. Just relax. I'm the pilot.

Reading Between the Lions

2 parts:
Expert – a bit of a know-all
Beginner – very nervous

Scene: *They are camping inside a small tent at night*

Beginner	What was that?
Expert	What?
Beginner	That noise.
Expert	Just the wind shaking the tent.
Beginner	Are you sure?
Expert	Yes. I'm a camping expert. Now slip into your sleeping bag and I'll switch off my torch.
Beginner	I want to read for a while.
Expert	It's very late.
Beginner	I know. It took us ages to put up this tent. But I want to read for a bit. It helps me to relax. What did you say?
Expert	Nothing.
Beginner	Yes you did. I heard a noise. A sort of grunt.

Expert	It's nothing. You'll get used to it. You've never been camping before. I'm an expert. I'm used to these things.
Beginner	Then why did you take so long to put up the tent?
Expert	It was dark. And I've never been here before.
Beginner	Is it meant to wobble like that?
Expert	What?
Beginner	The side of the tent. It just wobbled.
Expert	It's nothing – just the wind in the guy ropes. No problem.
Beginner	Does wind sniff?
Expert	Look, I know what I'm doing. Now get into your sleeping bag.
Beginner	It was a sniff and a scratching noise.
Expert	I told you – it's the rope flapping on the side of the tent.
Beginner	And a snort. I heard a loud snort!
Expert	Only a sheep. We're in parkland. You get used to all these sounds when you've camped as much as me. As I said, I'm an expert. You've got nothing to worry about if you're with me.
Beginner	This camp bed is a bit wobbly.

Expert	You'll get used to it.
Beginner	Pardon?
Expert	I said, 'You'll get used to it'.
Beginner	No. Not that. You made a silly noise. A hiss. A sort of rustle, then a snuffle.
Expert	Just the breeze in the trees. You read your book. Have my torch.
Beginner	Oh my word! That was a howl. I heard a horrible howl out there.
Expert	You've been reading too many horror stories.
Beginner	Have you done the guy ropes?
Expert	Don't worry. This tent is safe. I'm an expert. Leave it all to me.
Beginner	Then what was that scraping sound? As if the tent was ripping . . .
Expert	It's nothing. I told you – I know what I'm doing.
Beginner	There it was again – like something rubbing against the ropes. You must have heard it.
Expert	Yes – but it's just the noises of the night. I'm used to them.
Beginner	That was a thud. A loud thud. And a splutter and a plonk. Listen there's someone out there.

What shall we do?

Expert   You just read your book. What book is it, anyway?

Beginner   The Bible.

Expert   The Bible? What do you want that for when you're camping?

Beginner   Peace of mind.

Expert   Peace of mind? No harm can come to you when you're camping! Remember, I'm an expert. And let's face it, the Bible hasn't got anything in it about camping!

Beginner   Yes it has. It warns you to take care on the campsite.

Expert   Rubbish! Where does it say that?

Beginner   In Judges. It says in Chapter 4, Verse 21: 'She took a tent peg and a hammer and killed him by driving the peg right through his head and into the ground.' It does tend to put you off camping.

Expert   But that's just some old story. Nothing like that can happen here.

Beginner   Sssh! Listen. There was that noise again. Just like the sound of a tent peg being hammered into flesh . . .

Expert	Don't be daft. We're in a safe park, not some graveyard or jungle. That Bible has got nothing to tell me – I'm an expert.
Beginner	I think I just heard a growl.
Expert	Probably a train in the distance.
Beginner	What sort of park is this?
Expert	Very safe. It's one of those special parks.
Beginner	What do you mean?
Expert	Where they have a special theme. A theme park.
Beginner	What sort of theme?
Expert	Red Indians, I think. Westerns and all that. Horses and wigwams.
Beginner	Red Indians?
Expert	Yes. R.I. for short. I saw the sign.
Beginner	Sounds a bit odd to me!
Expert	This is a very safe R.I. park. The notice said so on the gates.
Beginner	What was that snarl?
Expert	Nothing. Remember, I'm an expert. It said it all on the notice.
Beginner	What did it say?

Expert	It said this is a SAFE R.I. PARK.
Beginner	Good. What was that? It sounded like a purr.
Expert	Relax, I'm the expert.
Beginner	Or more like a squawk. Anyway, there were three sets of gates we came through, an electric fence and all that wire.
Expert	I told you we're safe. It's to keep out all the yobs. Go to sleep.
Beginner	Gosh! You must have heard that!
Expert	Yes, I did!
Beginner	What did it sound like to you?
Expert	Just . . . a roar.
Beginner	Was it the wind?
Expert	No. It wasn't the wind. I've just thought . . . a horrible thought!
Beginner	I'm not worried. After all, you're the expert. I trust you.
Expert	I've just thought. It was the letter 'A'.
Beginner	What are you going on about? Oh, there it is again. That wind is really roaring now. It must be a storm about to start.
Expert	It isn't the wind. It's the notice I saw.

Beginner	What, the one about the safe R.I. park? How can that make a roar?
Expert	No. But it was an 'A' and not an 'E'.
Beginner	I don't follow you. Gosh! Just listen to that roar. It's just like thunder right outside the tent. Still, you're the expert.
Expert	It wasn't SAFE R.I. PARK, but . . . SAFARI PARK!
Beginner	Does it make any difference?
Expert	A safari park is where they have BEASTS! A zoo – with teeth!
Beginner	Just hark at that wind out there.
Expert	It isn't wind. They're on the loose. Our little tent is slap-bang in the middle of a field of lions! They're prowling all around us. I can hear their breath. I can feel their breath. I can smell their breath . . . and it smells of . . . hunger . . .
Beginner	So you think they're pretty close? After all, you're the expert.
Expert	No I'm not. I think I've made a little bodge-up! Oh gosh, look – there's a claw coming under the tent . . .
Beginner	Is it serious? I've got a tin of tuna in my rucksack. That might keep them happy.
Expert	I doubt it. Start praying. Get that Bible of yours open again.

Beginner	Oh look, there are teeth coming through the ground sheet.
Expert	Read out some words of comfort – quick!
Beginner	Which bit shall I read? Anyway, you said it was a waste of time.
Expert	Give it a try. Anything. Read something to give us hope.
Beginner	I'll just open it anywhere and read it out.
Expert	Look out, there's a face dribbling and chewing through the zip at the door! Start reading that Bible.
Beginner	Right. It's fallen open at Daniel . . .
Expert	Quick, read it out. We need all the help we can get. See what news God has for us . . . Just a bit of comfort . . .
Beginner	Here we go then . . . Chapter 6 and Verse 24 . . . 'And the lions jumped on them and broke all their bones . . . '
Expert	Fat lot of good you are. It's at times like this I wish I'd gone to church more often!

[Roar]

[Blackout]

[Crunch!]

Wrong Number

2 parts:

Mr Proctor, Mrs Yates

Scene: Mr Proctor *(from the repair shop) and a worried*
Mrs Yates *are speaking on the telephone.*

Proctor	Hello, is that 531627?

[*Pause*]

Proctor	Is that Mrs Gates?
Yates	Hello? This is 521637.
Proctor	Mrs Gates of Hill Mews?
Yates	Yes, Mrs Yates of Mill Views.
Proctor	This is Proctor's, the Repair Shop.
Yates	Sorry, who?
Proctor	About your washing machine . . .
Yates	What? I can't hear you.
Proctor	Proctor's
Yates	Oh, the doctor's. Good, I've been expecting you.
Proctor	Can you speak up a bit?
Yates	I've been expecting you.
Proctor	Yes, what seems to be the trouble?

Yates	I told you once. I phoned this morning.
Proctor	I'm afraid our tea boy dropped the note pad in the sink and lost all our messages. We're in a bit of a mess at the moment.
Yates	It's just as well I wasn't in need of the kiss of life, then.
Proctor	Well, he's a dab hand with a foot pump and a G clamp.
Yates	This is not a joking matter.
Proctor	Right. Tell me what the trouble is so I can bring the right tools.
Yates	The what?
Proctor	What seems to be the problem?
Yates	It's the same as last time, I'm afraid.
Proctor	Oh – and what was that?
Yates	Well, you should know. It should be on my card.
Proctor	Oh yes, I remember. You'd sprung a leak.
Yates	No I hadn't. It was a very bad cold.
Proctor	Did you say cold?
Yates	Yes. Not very nice at all. My head was spinning and I was as white as a sheet.

Proctor	I see. So the water's not heating and not spinning the sheets.
Yates	I beg your pardon?
Proctor	Hot water is a problem, is it?
Yates	No, I had a hot bath this morning, but as I was letting the water out I came over all swimmy.
Proctor	Must be the pump packing up.
Yates	You mean my heart? Should I take something for it?
Proctor	How do you mean?
Yates	A nip of brandy or something. It could be the start of flu. My insides aren't too good, either.
Proctor	Sorry? I'm not quite with you. Did you say something about the insides?
Yates	Yes. A bit dodgy.
Proctor	Making noises?
Yates	Well yes, a bit.
Proctor	What sort of noises?
Yates	Sort of rumbling.
Proctor	When? During the final rinse?
Yates	No – just before meals.
Proctor	Does something sound loose?

Yates	Loose? What do you mean, loose?
Proctor	As if something has come away from the body.
Yates	Come away from the body? Like what?
Proctor	A nut or bolt. Maybe some part has worn through. What sort of powder do you use?
Yates	Powder? Talcum powder from Boots.
Proctor	Boots? You don't wash boots in it, do you? They could dent the drum.
Yates	The drum? What, the ear drum? So it could be my ears? Could it be wax?
Proctor	Maybe. It might need a bit of wax on the drive arm.
Yates	The arm? But my arm seems fine.
Proctor	Or the spinner neck.
Yates	Well yes, my neck is a bit stiff.
Proctor	What sort is it?
Yates	My neck? The normal sort. The sort that keeps the head on the shoulders. I've got a bit of sunburn on it.
Proctor	Is it a Hot Point?
Yates	Well yes, pretty warm at times. It could be the way I slept on it.

Proctor	You slept on it? You slept on the washing machine? Does that help?
Yates	Did you say sleeping on the washing machine will help? I must try it!
Proctor	What about dropping off?
Yates	Can't you give me some sleeping pills to help? Will it get better?
Proctor	Hard to tell. I'll be able to tell once I get my hands in there and feel around the pipes.
Yates	You what?
Proctor	I'll get in the back. You probably need a bit of a clean up and some oil. How old are things now?
Yates	Well I don't like to say on the phone . . . 43 last week.
Proctor	43 . . . Don't be daft. That's much too old to be any good.
Yates	You mean there's no hope?
Proctor	Not at that age. I can't get the spare parts.
Yates	Spare parts? You don't mean to say bits might need replacing?
Proctor	Of course. They don't last long these days.
Yates	So it could be a transplant, then?

Proctor	There's a lot of wear and tear.
Yates	But I don't smoke or anything.
Proctor	Did you say smoke?
Yates	Yes.
Proctor	Where? It's not coming out of the sides, is it?
Yates	No.
Proctor	That's a relief. Last week I had to see a woman with suds squirting out of the tubes, smoke pouring out of the back end and sparks shooting out of the bottom. Not a pretty sight.
Yates	You don't think I'm going the same way, do you?
Proctor	Hard to tell. You might just need the belt tightened.
Yates	Yes I have lost a bit of weight.
Proctor	When did you last have your filter scrubbed?
Yates	I don't know. I had my tonsils out as a child.
Proctor	It might just need a bit of oil.
Yates	Oil? You mean caster oil?
Proctor	Have you been well-oiled lately?
Yates	Well, only at Christmas when I had a dash too much gin and orange.
Proctor	Then it could be rust.

Yates	Rust? Surely not.
Proctor	You must have your joints greased from time to time, you know.
Yates	How do you mean?
Proctor	All moving parts need a spot of grease every so often.
Yates	Oh. I never thought of that.
Proctor	It's amazing how much dust and dirt can get inside and clog up the works, you know.
Yates	So what can you do about it?
Proctor	No problem. It can all be sucked out with a Hoover. I just pop a tube through the front doo-dah, switch on and hope for the best.
Yates	Does it hurt?
Proctor	Oh no. In fact the last person was thrilled.
Yates	Thrilled?
Proctor	Yes. I sucked out a dead mouse, a tangled vest, half a custard cream, three cuff-links and a soggy five pound note.
Yates	No! But where from?
Proctor	All blocked up in the outlet pipe.
Yates	So what do you think I ought to do for the best?

Proctor	Just switch off and wait for me to come round for a bit of a potter about. I'll just delve around here and there. You could just fill up with water. That would save time. I'm on my way right now. I'm using my mobile phone in my van.
Yates	Fill up with water? How much?
Proctor	To the brim.
Yates	To the brim? Hot or cold?
Proctor	The hotter the better – with plenty of soap. Or better still, a bit of bleach.
Yates	Are you sure? I'll try to swallow all I can but I'll have to go for a lie down. I'll leave the door unlocked. Let yourself in.
Proctor	I've got my drill, saw and screw-driver so don't worry.
Yates	I'm dreading this, doctor. Are you sure it won't hurt?
Proctor	It can't do much harm. It sounds as if I might be able to rip a few bits out for scrap.
Yates	Scrap? It's my body you are talking about! I knew the Health Service would come to this. What about . . . my remains?

Proctor	No problem. I'll bung them in the skip. The scrap men might want to pick things over. You might get a few quid.
Yates	I don't know what to say.
Proctor	Don't mention it. All part of the service.
Yates	The funeral service? Can my ashes be scattered in the park?
Proctor	Ashes? We don't burn the left-overs any more. I just dump them in a tip by the gas works.
Yates	In a tip? What a way to go!
Proctor	Ah, here I am – outside your house.
Yates	Come straight in the back door.
Proctor	At least that great big dog of yours will be locked up!
Yates	The what?
Proctor	I know you wouldn't let anyone in unless that big pit-bull was locked away. I'm just coming in the kitchen now.
Yates	I haven't got a dog. Are you still outside? I can't see you through my window. I can't hear you down there.
Proctor	There's a funny growling noise.

Yates	I can just see your van from my window. It's parked outside Hill Mews down the road. That's where Mrs Gates lives with her huge dog.
Proctor	Oh blimey . . . help . . . pull it off. Aah, get it off my leg!
Yates	I've never felt so happy in all my life! I'm saved!
Proctor	Aaaaaaaaaaaaah!
Yates	It's all been a joke! You've been pulling my leg, haven't you?
Proctor	Not as much as he's pulling mine . . . Oh no . . . down boy . . . no AAH!

[*Crunch!*]